The All-American

Outhouse

Stories, Design & Construction

by Bob Cary,
American Society of
Outhouse Architects (A.S.O.A.)

Adventure Publications, Inc.
Cambridge, MN

1

Dedication:

I dedicate this book to my wife Edith who has traveled with me over much of the north country and has been my companion on canoe trails, hiking trails, ski trails and trails to an uncounted number of outhouses in the United States and Canada. In addition, she provided numerous insights into the use of such outdoor facilities recalled from her days as a young woman on the farm in Indiana.

Acknowledgments:

This book is the result of a team effort, much as the fact that you cannot produce a functional outhouse without a lumber yard for wood and shingles, a hardware store for seats, hinges and paint, and a paper mill for the end product.

Book and cover design by Jonathan Norberg

Blueprints by Steven H. McNeill, American Society of Outhouse Architects

Illustrations and photos by Bob Cary

Copyright 2003 by Bob Cary
Published by Adventure Publications, Inc.
820 Cleveland Street South
Cambridge, MN 55008
1-800-678-7006
All rights reserved
Printed in the United States of America
ISBN 1-59193-011-1

The All-American

Outhouse

Stories, Design & Construction

One of George's prodigious privies.

Preface

Over some 80 years of life, almost entirely spent in rural areas, the author has acquired extensive, firsthand knowledge of the location, planning, construction and utility of outhouses. He has had the good fortune to associate with experts in the field, skilled craftsmen who built for comfort and durability. These artisans generously shared their knowledge, particularly those details that might not be apparent to the unpracticed eye.

"Anyone," it is said, "can build an outhouse, but not everyone can build a good outhouse."

Those readers in the process of constructing or remodeling an outhouse are urged to place a copy of this treatise within easy reach of anyone using the present facility so that a careful study may be made concerning the information contained herein...sitting down, of course.

Table of Contents

Historical Perspective

In the history of our nation, at least the portion that is written, there is ample reference to forts, churches, capitols, meeting houses, universities, prisons, hostelries and various other edifices that have assumed the identity of shrines. There is even a substantial body of information, indeed whole libraries, concerning the preparation of food and drink for consumption since colonial times, but relatively little in the handling of that same material after being processed through the human digestive tract.

The Founding Fathers of this nation, devout churchgoers that they were, no doubt noted that from the time of Adam and through the parables of the loaves and fishes, frequent reference was made in the Scriptures concerning a divine Providence supplying food and drink for the multitudes, but silence in the realm of toilet use. It is almost as though it never occurred. However, the patriots of the thirteen colonies were aware, as we are today, that there are certain functions of the body that require—indeed sometimes scream out—for attention.

Brick toilets, by George! The outhouse had a position of prominence in early times, along with its equally utilitarian accessory, the chamber pot or "Thunder Mug." Preservation and restoration of various national historic sites, if done with authenticity, reveal the presence of both. Mount Vernon, that revered former homesite of our first president, George Washington, has been maintained in superb condition by the Mount Vernon Ladies' Association, purchased from Washington's descendants in 1858. Meticulous attention has been paid to detail, including the two brick outhouses of three-holer design. Each unit has two large holes and a small, children's hole in-between, for what might be termed "family togetherness."

They don't make 'em like they used to

As with most things associated with Washington, these edifices are substantial, painted white, and fit in with the general architecture. Indeed, if one does not know what these two buildings are, they might be passed over as seed houses or storage facilities for garden tools. Like the other buildings, they are constructed of colonial brick, which may have spawned the original observation often applied to something durable, to wit: "solid as a brick outhouse."

When one views these trim, six-sided buildings, it is quickly apparent they have the appearance of permanence. Obviously, they were not built to be moved. Unlike those wooden outhouses popular with less affluent dwellers who simply moved the facility to a new site when the hole was filled, George's brick toilets were designed to be emptied daily by slaves who pulled out wooden drawers from the back. The removed material was then dumped on the garden and used as fertilizer. Thus Mount Vernon was engaged in recycling more than 200 years before the term was invented.

Other well-to-do folks with permanent outhouses paid for the services of contractors who were known as honey dippers. These independent operators cleaned out the holes, bucket by bucket, and dumped the material into horse-drawn vats on wheels, which were hauled to farm land for fertilizer or the Potomac River and dumped. Indeed, even today, government officials are struggling to keep irresponsible citizens from using the Potomac as a sewer.

The chamber pot—friend or foe? Each bedroom in Mount Vernon was equipped with a crock chamber pot. Members of the household—George, Martha, children by her previous marriage and overnight guests—used the chamber pots at night, which eliminated the necessity of a trip outdoors in the dark, a touch of hospitality no doubt deeply appreciated by visitors. Each morning, the chambermaids would carry the full pots downstairs to the back door where they would be transported by other servants to the garden, emptied and rinsed. It was all handled with circumspection and dispatch.

Chamber pots were in general use throughout the colonies, although most people filled and emptied their own. In cities, they were often emptied into the gutter in the street outside the home or hostelry, which no doubt resulted in a somewhat pervasive aroma. In some instances, full chamber pots became weapons. It was known that in Philadelphia, on that fatefully hot July of 1776, when the Second Continental Congress was debating the Declaration of Independence, there were, among the citizenry, a number of British Loyalists who boldly made their views known. It has been reported that several of the more eloquent street orators, while loudly proclaiming the benefits of British rule, were hit from second story windows by full chamber pot loads. Indeed, it was somewhat chancy, even under the best circumstances, to stride the streets of many communities in the morning when pots were being emptied.

MY OWN MEMORIES OF CHAMBER POTS
go back some 70 years to my summer vacations, sometimes spent as an indentured servant for my Aunt Nellie who had a summer cottage on the Fox River. For most emergencies, we trekked from the cottage to the adjacent outhouse, some 100 yards to the east, but when the weather was frightful, particularly at night, Aunt Nellie preferred the chamber pot. It was one of my duties, with the arrival of daylight, to carry the pot by its wire handle to the outhouse and dump the contents down the hole. I then sloshed it with a couple of buckets of soapy water and left it upside down outside to dry. I recall that it was a glazed receptacle, about 16 inches in height, white, with an assortment of red and blue flowers tastefully baked into the finish.

OF MORE RECENT MEMORY was a combination outhouse and chemical toilet my family used the first winter we moved into the north country, in 1966. Some fifty yards uphill from the log cabin was the outhouse, quite functional during the summer months. However, when winter approached, my wife and teenage daughter insisted on a more comfortable indoor facility and we settled on a chemical unit. It consisted of a regular toilet seat that was located over a tank. Inside the tank was a ten-gallon galvanized bucket with a chemical that rendered the deposited material nearly odor-free. We placed it in a small room near the bedrooms and it worked exceptionally well with a single drawback: It had to be emptied about every four days. That is, I carried the ten gallons of material uphill to the outhouse and dumped it down the hole, then returned to the cabin and recharged the unit with a gallon of fresh water and chemical.

All went well until late in the winter. The toilet worked to perfection. The only problem was, my scheduled trips to the outhouse resulted in the path through the hip-deep snow acquiring an increasingly treacherous coat of ice.

One day in late March, with the sun high, the temperature in the high forties and the path a slick, wet chute, it happened. Halfway up the hill, fighting for balance, my boots slipped out from under me and I made a grandiose, arm-flailing, terror-stricken flop. As I went down, certain of a fate worse than death, I attempted one last, desperate lunge, brought the bucket overhead and managed to land on my back with the bucket falling a few feet downhill where it clanged and banged its way back to the cabin, strewing its contents all along the path. With a prayer of thanks for my deliverance, I covered the old path with snow and shoveled a new path to the outhouse, something I should have done earlier, finishing the winter without further incident.

The "modern" outhouse

Outhouses, over generations, have earned a significant place in American life, albeit with an occasional snicker and unwarranted jest. Alas, the advent of indoor plumbing, sparked by British physician Dr. John Crapper's invention of the flush toilet, nearly spelled doom to the venerable outhouse, but not entirely. In more remote areas of the hinterland, the outhouse has, fortunately, held its ground. And now, as a new generation of urban Americans, buoyed by financial success, seek out sites for summer retreats along rivers and lakeshore, the historic sanitary edifice of our fore-fathers is enjoying a new resurgence of popularity.

In conjunction with this outdoor migration, the younger generation has discovered something they term "the environment" and seeks ways to lessen the human impact upon the planet. The outhouse, it can be argued, is the most environmentally cor-rect device ever developed for disposing of human waste. It requires no water, no electrical energy, no plastic or copper plumbing, no sewers to overflow or rupture and it pollutes no river.

That is, if properly sited and built. Unfortunately, many of the e-mail set, while well informed in home design, haven't a clue as to how an outdoor toilet should be located, designed, constructed and used.

Those of us who are senior members of the socie-ty, elders of the tribe, as it were, with outhouse knowledge gained from long association, have a patriotic duty to instruct our descendants in this important facet of rural living. And they, in turn, can hopefully preserve this vital aspect of leg-endary American life for future generations in the land of the free and the home of the brave.

Selecting the Site

Sure, it's big enough, but look at the location! Location of the outhouse is of critical importance if it is to adequately provide for the services intended. One has only to watch the TV screen when a flood is in progress to note the number of outdoor toilets hurtling along on the turbulence along with chicken coops and other flotsam. Obviously, no outhouse should be built on lowland, particularly on a river floodplain. One need not build on a mountain top, but high, dry ground is preferable.

THERE IS A BACK COUNTRY TALE of an old farmer who lived adjacent to a large river, a man with unshakable religious faith. He was on his way to the outhouse when a neighbor in a pickup truck drove into the farm yard and shouted: "Henry! There's been a cloudburst upriver and the dam may break. Jump in the truck and I'll get you out of here!"

"No!" the old man yelled back. "I have faith the Lord will protect me. I'm staying right here!"

Unfortunately, the dam broke and the river rose over the floor of the outhouse. Another neighbor came by, this one in a motorboat, and saw the farmer peering out of the outhouse door. "Wade out here, Henry!" he yelled. "I can save you!"

"No!" the old farmer shouted back. "I have faith the Lord will take care of me. I'm staying right here!"

A half hour later, the farmer was on top of the outhouse roof with the raging waters swirling around. A state rescue helicopter appeared overhead and spotting the old man, the pilot hovered above. "I can see you down there!"

he yelled over a bullhorn. "I will drop you a rope with a loop on the end. Put it around your body and I will pull you to safety!"

"No! No!" The farmer yelled back. "I have faith the Lord will take care of me!"

At this point, the raging torrent swept away the outhouse and the farmer, who was drowned.

A short time later, the farmer found himself in heaven. "Lord!" he cried out in anguish. "I have been a devout believer all my life. When the flood came, I had faith you would save me. What happened?"

"What happened?" retorted the Lord, shaking His head. "Henry, I sent a guy in a pickup truck, a guy in a motor-boat and a guy in a helicopter. What made you refuse the help?"

———————————

A drive down the back roads of rural America reveals historic farmsteads inevitably sited on hills, house and outhouse together. One gains the impression that our pioneering ancestors were considerably smarter about home location than the present generation. They didn't need flood insurance.

*Breeze &
the slippery
slope*
Before one spade of earth is turned, before a single nail is hammered, a careful assessment of the property should be undertaken to determine the optimum site. Old time builders were apt to seat themselves on a handy stump and study the area thoughtfully at length, taking into consideration, for one, the direction of the prevailing wind. Obviously, the focus would then be concentrated

upon that area downwind from the house or cabin.

Where the property is sloping, the outhouse site is also best located downhill from the house and, particularly, the well. Reasons for this should not require a detailed explanation. "Locating the outhouse near or uphill from the well," one grizzled old builder pointed out, "is often in bad taste."

Admittedly, there may be impediments to proper siting, such as a proximity to lakeshore, river bank, stone ledge or dense forest. County zoning laws usually spell out shoreline setbacks. One must take care to adhere to county codes and, above all, secure the proper building permits if required.

Can you dig it?

Trained outhouse architects generally prefer a site on a gentle slope 100 feet to the lee of the house and adjacent to or screened by a grove of saplings or woody shrubs to ensure privacy. Lilacs make a superb screen and add a pleasing aroma when in flower. A row of balsams will do admirably. But such pastoral considerations are dependent upon the geology...what lies below the surface. What sometimes appears to be the most desirable site may not be digable. Where my wife and I dwell in Northeastern Minnesota, our property is largely underlaid with what scientists term "The Canadian Shield," impervious granite, greenstone and gabbro, two billion years old and often just a few feet to a few inches under the sod. This can pose a considerable impediment in excavating the hole.

Let us say the location selected appears level, grassy, screened from view and is the correct distance and direction from the house. Without expending a prodigious amount of exploratory digging, how can one be certain what lies below?

Certainly, it is possible to attack the earth with pick and shovel, hoping for the best but risking the chance of slamming the pick into bedrock with bone-jarring impact.

The experienced site engineer is more likely to use about five feet of 5/8" steel reinforcing rod, sharpened to a point on one end so it can be driven into the turf within the area selected as the site. If the rod strikes solid rock, it can be pulled up and driven in a foot or two to one side to determine if the obstruction is solid ledge or merely a large rock in the rubble below. By moving the rod around and driving it down several times, one may determine the suitability of the site. Once a digable area is discovered, serious excavation may commence.

Welcome to the country, here's your shovel

A depth of five or six feet is quite adequate, although some prefer an extra foot and some are satisfied with a four-foot hole. Obviously, the deeper the hole, the longer it lasts. Moving an outhouse is an undertaking with its own hazards.

Accidentally falling into the pit is obviously an experience to be avoided. It has happened, however, with results often dire.

MY FATHER OFTEN RECALLED the instance when a nearby neighbor was replacing an ancient outhouse with a new one in early spring and while setting the floor joists, slipped on the wet clay and fell into the pit.

Choking and floundering about in the mess, he discovered the sides of the pit were too slippery to climb out. He began to shout "Fire! Fire!" at the top of his lungs, bringing his wife and sons racing from the farmhouse. In short order they shoved a ladder into the hole and the old man clambered out.

As his wife was hosing him off, she inquired, "Silas, tell me why in the world you were yelling 'Fire! Fire!'"

"I didn't think," the farmer said, "that anyone would come running to help if I started to yell 'Poop!'"

Another important consideration concerns trees. Small saplings and shrubs pose no insurmountable problems; but large trees, while providing welcome shade, may have systems of large roots just below the surface. Roots tend to extend the same distance horizontally underground as the tree trunk extends above ground. Single roots may be chopped through but a maze of roots may require seeking an alternate site.

It can be readily seen that location is far from simple. So is digging the hole. If the outhouse is a 4x6 two-holer, the excavation should come just inside that by perhaps a half foot on all sides, like 3x5. This allows for a rim of solid earth upon which the foundation may rest. More on this later. When actually digging, one will note that the first few feet down are relatively easy, even for a rank amateur with a shovel. But after four feet below ground level, digging becomes infinitely more difficult. The average hole requires excavating about 144 cubic feet of earth, or somewhere in excess of 700 shovels full that must be loosened with a pick or with a downward thrust of the spade and hurled out at waist or shoulder height. This has been known to cause severe back strain among elderly builders and even some of the younger set. If there is a construction project going on in the neighborhood it is often worthwhile to contact a backhoe operator and have him spend an hour or so excavating the outhouse hole. It is money well spent.

How low(land) can you go? Oh, one more thing. Locating an outhouse in a swampy lowland can create serious problems. If the site is not well-drained, the hole may fill with water. Cold water. The human material dropping into the hole may fail to decompose, may instead pile up excessively and create a horrendous odor. Also, a good load released from above may hit with such force as to send a small geyser back up, splashing the underside of the person seated. Nothing will destroy an individual's concentration quicker than icy water hitting a delicate part of one's anatomy.

In summary, a happy family is a family with a well-drained, conveniently-located, functional outhouse.

Architectural Planning

George Washington's outhouse at Mount Vernon. Fancy, but functional.

Even a cursory drive up the back roads of rural America reveals an infinite number of outhouse designs. Many of these are, unfortunately, no longer in use, since much of the farming community has adopted some modification of the flush invention of Dr. John Crapper, the eminent British bathroom plumbing expert. Thus one may see scores of abandoned outdoor toilet facilities, some kept on the farmstead for sentimental reasons or simply because the owner didn't get around to knocking it over.

Be that as it may, it is readily apparent that a few existing facilities exhibit exceptional design and some are serviceable though lacking in artistic conception; but many are a disgrace, a blot upon the landscape. One thrust of this tome is an attempt to correct such misdirected effort. For the sake of simplicity, this book concentrates on three distinct models, each created for a specific segment of society.

The Economy One-Holer

It's a starter model

This is the basic, no-frills, single hole model preferred by bachelors, elderly maiden school teachers, first-time cabin builders and small families. For this facility, a simple 4x4 floor plan is ample, easy to construct and allows for maximum use of stock-sized lumber.

Admittedly, a 4x6 floor plan is roomier and exhibits a certain aura of optimism, such as the possibility that the bachelor intends to acquire a wife and expand to a two-holer. Or the family may achieve the American dream, climb the ladder of success, perhaps even hit the lottery and opt for a more luxurious facility.

The 4x4 model features a flat roof, sloping from about 7 feet, 6 inches in front to 5 feet, 6 inches in the back. This slope is so rainfall drips off the rear and not down the person's neck at the entrance. Eaves should extend at least a half foot on all sides, perhaps a foot over the door in front. In any event, even the most modest one-holer should be constructed sturdily with thought and pride.

Timber!

In many instances, we have seen outhouses made of scrap lumber, odds and ends of cracked and split boards, ancient pine with knot holes and random lengths, all of which invite leakage, cold winter drafts and ingress by small rodents and myriad noxious insects. Poor lumber may also allow the building to lean out of plumb so the door will fail to close tightly. Let it be clear that there is nothing wrong with used lumber, but it should be sound and free of nails, holes and other serious blemishes.

To digress a moment, there may be occasions when an outhouse is deliberately designed and built out-of-plumb. Such an instance occurred on

Highway 1, south of my home town of Ely, Minnesota, heading toward Lake Superior and Grand Marais. That twisty stretch of road is frequented more by moose than motorists and there are few oases of comfort along the way. Thus it was that a Mr. K (who preferred anonymity) had some years ago constructed a fine one-holer between his house and the road, the best site on the property.

Unfortunately, passing motorists in desperate straits developed a habit of stopping, jumping from their cars and racing to the new outhouse for relief. In frustration, Mr. K tore down his facility and immediately rebuilt, only this time with a bizarre 30-degree slant to the walls. Although solidly built, the edifice appeared to be in imminent danger of collapse and promptly lost favor with the motoring public.

Best seat in the house The seat should be boxed in solidly, preferably of smooth plywood, with a one-piece front splash board. Some careless builders have been known to hastily nail up splash boards of several odd pieces of plank. This inevitably results in cracks, which may widen in time and cause spatters on the floor of the outhouse if not on the back of one's shoes.

The hole shape can be marked by having one's wife seated comfortably on the plywood top with her panties down. In this position the perimeter of her bottom may be conveniently scribed with a heavy pencil. Next, the actual hole size is marked about two inches inside the scribed perimeter. Within that, a hole is drilled to accommodate the saber saw used to cut out the seat.

In general, an adult seat will run about 8 inches wide and 11 ½ inches front to back. Size is of utmost importance. Too large, and a skinny person may slip down and become wedged in the hole. Too small, and an individual in haste may skid to one side or the other, winding up completely off target. Also, large holes can be a definite hazard to small children. Kids will oft times attempt to emulate their parents, climbing up to use a seat too large. The answer is a separate, custom-built hole for the little ones, but more on that later.

Once a hole is sawn to shape, it should be tested by the intended user, touched up with a rasp to provide a comfortable fit and sanded velvety smooth. There is nothing that destroys tranquility and wrecks a person's concentration like a splinter in a tender spot.

Rather than centered on the cover, the hole may be offset to provide shelf space for toilet paper, reading material, crossword puzzles or another hole, if a two-holer becomes necessary.

Before construction is suspended, a suitable hole cover should be installed. A rectangular wooden lid, perhaps two inches larger than the hole and equipped with a simple lift handle, will suffice. A hinged cover is preferred by many discriminating builders, the cover tilting and braced to form a convenient back rest when the seat is in use.

For ease in cleaning, all wooden parts of seats should be either enameled, or, if a wood grain finish is preferred, given two coats of polyurethane. Very young boys and very old men, in particular, occasionally exhibit atrocious marksmanship.

**Give them
some air!**

Lastly, ventilation must be taken into account. Old time outhouses had designs cut into the door for air circulation. Preferred patterns included the half moon, cloverleaf and entwined hearts, the latter a romantic touch preferred by newlyweds. Tradition has kept these more or less on the market but newer units are now equipped with four-inch PVC vent pipes that originate under the seat, go up one side and exit above the roof, carrying off much of the formerly offensive aroma.

The pipe should have a "T" cap on top to keep out rain or snow, and screened to discourage bats from going down the pipe. You haven't seen utter terror until you've experienced a bat loose in an outhouse at night.

Traditional Two-Holer

Through the test of experience, rural America discovered early on that occasions arise when two people have to use the outhouse at the same time. Thus we have the double-seat facility allowing for such emergencies, obviously superior to many modern urban homes with a single bathroom and one toilet.

His & hers It is a heartwarming sight to see newlyweds, by dawn's early light, tripping up to the two-holer, hand-in-hand, starting off the day with romantic togetherness.

There are instances, however, when one or both of the recently wed couple may be afflicted with a measure of bashfulness and prefer to endure considerable discomfort, if not pain, until the outhouse is vacant. Poor timing can result in a young wife shivering disconsolately outside in the wind and sleet while hubby is inside comfortably reading *Sports Illustrated*.

Untimely divorce can be averted simply by erecting a dividing wall between the holes and installing two doors with one marked MEN and the other designated WOMEN. Occasionally, one runs across divided two-holers where the owner has engaged in a fling of whimsy, the door signs perhaps reading BUCKS and DOES, DRAKES and HENS, BULLS and HEIFERS, etc. Such attempts at levity may be worth a brief chuckle while en route.

Affording a two-holer usually indicates the owner has reached an economic plateau where other improvements may be enjoyed. Probably the most important upgrade is the installation of a genuine commercial-type toilet seat, purchased from the local hardware store. Not only are they usually more comfortable than a sawn hole and easier to maintain, but they come in a variety of hues adding a cheerful note to what might be an otherwise mundane interior. Also, the walls may be painted to complement the seat color, or vice versa, providing an element of charm and originality.

Windows to the world

Over generations, there have been outhouse architects who advocated the use of windows for interior illumination. We have never seen the cost-effectiveness of these. Windows require curtains or they will assuredly invite would-be users to peek in, particularly if they find the door shut and wonder if the unit is really occupied. And windows invite rocks thrown by irresponsible urchins. Show me an outhouse with a busted window and I'll show you a near-useless facility, especially during the mosquito season.

And it's good for them too!

Additionally, the two-holer is recognized as an important training tool for children of new parents, providing hands-on education in potty use. There is a feeling of warmth when one witnesses a mother and small child wending hand-in-hand up a flower-rimmed path to the outhouse on a sunlit day with butterflies drifting over the greensward and a throng of songbirds providing an a cappella chorus in the background. Such an excursion not only introduces the youngster to a necessary function of civilized life, but can instill important rudiments of independence and self confidence.

Most two-holers are constructed to accommodate two adults, but one hole can be modified for a small child. The hole, of necessity, is scribed and sawn considerably smaller to fit the individual. A seven-inch movable step can be built so it may be skidded over to the toilet when a youngster enters. Since a standard height for an adult seat is 15 inches, a youth potty functions best with eight-inch legroom thus the seven-inch step will bridge the gap. As the youngster grows older and legs inevitably lengthen, the step can be lowered and then discarded altogether as the child reaches about seventh grade.

A word of warning here: When not in use, the movable step should be stored to one side.

OUR NEIGHBOR, EDDIE KLOTZ, said he had a carpenter come out to install a new seat in his outhouse and coming into the darkened interior from bright sunlight, didn't see the kids' step and stumbled over it, falling with a crash. Eddie came running at the bang in time to meet the carpenter emerging, red-faced and swearing up a storm.

"You got a fish pole I can borrow?" the carpenter yelled.

"Yeah, I got a fish pole, but what for?"

"I stumbled over that damn kids' step," the carpenter snarled, "and when I fell, I dropped my jacket down the hole. I need the fish pole to hook it out."

"Well, the jacket won't be any good now," Eddie pointed out.

"I know," groaned the carpenter, "but I've got my lunch in the pocket."

The Deluxe Sun Roof Three-Holer

Lifestyles of the rich & rustic

This is the very pinnacle of outhouse design, an elegant status symbol of rural aristocracy. One need only refer to George Washington's three-holers at Mount Vernon or Thomas Jefferson's three-holers at Monticello as examples of architectural three-seat superiority.

The current sun roof option, a relatively recent feature, provides maximum illumination without sacrificing one iota of privacy. The sun roof may be a commercial skylight purchased from a builder's supply or it may be an auto sunroof removed with a cutting torch from the metal top of a pre-driven junk yard sports car. In all cases, extreme care must be taken to install the unit with a tight fit against rainwater seepage. Most outhouse owners with any type of skylight are advised to install a sign directing users to close same when leaving. Roof openings invite invasion by bees, wasps and hornets, any of which may constitute a distraction when one is engaged in quiet contemplation.

Popular in recent years has been the use of translucent fiberglass paneled roofs. These are relatively inexpensive, can be had in a variety of colors and allow diffused light through the entire roof. There are only two slight drawbacks: In the summer, considerable heat penetrates to the interior and it is noisy in a sleet or heavy rainstorm.

Elbow room

A 4x6 floor plan will accommodate a three-hole facility, but 4x8 is decidedly roomier and more impressive. A large family, indicative of the population explosion, may require a four-holer with two adult and two juvenile seats, the latter sawn from seven to ten inches to accommodate a range of growing youngsters. Dividing walls may accord gender privacy, adult and juvenile males on one side, adult and juvenile females on the other.

There was a report sent in that the outhouse at the Old Armstrong Lake Resort had a sketch showing the outhouse with slots on both sides and a plank with various holes of different sizes sawn along its length. The theory was, the occupant could slide the board along and try out the holes until he found a perfect fit, then use it with contentment.

Customize! In a large unit, two PVC vent pipes are recommended, one on the men's side, one on the women's. A thoughtful touch on the women's side might be fluffy nylon pile seat covers. Sage or taupe are "in" colors this year.

In remote wilderness regions we have seen both women's and men's seats covered with thick beaver fur, but this has tended to create environmental controversy, drawing criticism from animal protectionists.

One of the more sumptuous outhouses in the Section 30 area is the 8x8 electrically heated, thermostat-controlled (60 degree) facility owned by Roger and Karla Doppelhammer. The unit boasts a 3x5 picture window with curtains, book cases, pictures on the walls and an exhaust fan that pushes warm air down the hole and out a vent in the roof.

An upgrade might include screen exterior doors swinging outward while the interior doors swing in. This allows a modicum of light and ventilation without encouraging an insect invasion.

The door swings both ways

When upgrading doors, another consideration involves privacy and door closures. This hinges on whether the door opens inward or outward. The inward school of thought holds that if your mother is seated comfortably with the door open a slight crack for light and ventilation, she only has to push the door shut with her foot if she hears footsteps on the path. On the other hand, an inward door is sometimes awkward when entering. Doors that swing outward offer more room and are easy to install. However, they have the disadvantage of allowing intrusion. A good interior latch is essential, otherwise someone coming in a hurry and not knowing the facility is occupied can jerk the door open and, well, there you are.

While you can select your own door arrangement, you have no control over someone else's. There will surely come a time when you pull open an outward-swinging door and discover some astonished individual sitting inside. My father, a gentleman and authority on rural diplomacy, instructed me at an early age that if such an incident occurred and I found myself staring at a blushing female, my course of action was to immediately avert my eyes, say "Excuse me, SIR!" and quickly slam the door. This gives the victim a sense that the intruder didn't get a good look at her and assumed it was a man on the seat. And it allows for a hasty but dignified retreat without screams for help and accusations of moral turpitude.

Accessories

All the
extras

There is a saying that an outhouse is just a building until it is fully equipped. Toilet paper and means for dispensing it is of critical importance. A regular white plastic tissue holder is serviceable but a wrought iron or brass holder adds a distinct flair, particularly when accompanied by matching wrought iron or brass door hardware and magazine rack. One may, of course, go overboard on furnishings.

OUR FRIEND CLAIRE BELL RELATES
that her family once purchased a summer cottage near Ishpeming, in Michigan's Upper Peninsula, complete with a rustic outhouse. At one point in time, her father had inherited a full-length wall mirror and having no other place to install it, hung it on the inside of the outhouse door. Thus family members, when seated, elbows on knees, had the somewhat unique experience of seeing themselves in lifelike reflection, staring back, elbows on knees.

Claire recalls that as a very young child, she once ventured alone to the facility, managed to scramble up on the seat and prepared to take care of the problem at hand. As she stared in fascination at her image on the mirror she was suddenly horrified to see the image of a huge pine snake emerge from the back of the seat and begin a sinuous climb toward the roof.

"I screamed," said Claire, "bolted from the outhouse and ran, screaming and screaming, to the cottage. I do not recall if I completed my mission, but I do know that it was a couple of years before they could get me to use that outhouse and only then if someone went with me."

Mirror aside, that incident is an example of what can happen when construction is not precise and openings are allowed to appear in the walls.

Also, when siding is not tight-fitting, such creatures as squirrels or chipmunks may find their way inside. What they invariably do is eat a hole through the roll of paper. They don't chew on the ends, they gnaw right through the middle, rendering at least every other sheet useless. Old timers didn't use paper holders for that reason, preferring to keep their roll of paper under a coffee can next to the seat.

Toilet paper's prestigious ancestry

Toilet paper itself is a relatively recent invention. Possibly the first toilet tissue consisted of near-worthless Continental script paid the American troops during the Revolution. "Not worth a Continental" was a common saying, but it may not have applied to its use in the latrines.

Of course, there have been any number of products used as paper substitutes. Very early in life, many of us old timers recall a wooden box of corn cobs in the outhouse on the farm. Soft, fuzzy corncobs performed an adequate service and cost nothing. My grandfather occasionally remarked that the more affluent farmers had two boxes, one with brown cobs and one with white cobs.

"They used a brown cob diligently," Grandfather observed. "Then they used a white cob to see if they needed another brown cob."

Probably the most famous outhouse tissues in our nation were provided by Sears Roebuck & Co. catalogs. The Sears catalog not only furnished useful paper but was a source of educational reading material. Many a farm boy gained his first intimate knowledge of female anatomy by perusing the women's lingerie pages in the Sears book as he sat in the outhouse. Pages used as tissue were torn out as they were read. City folk usually did not know that catalog pages had to be crumpled and then smoothed out. Rural folk knew crumpling gave each sheet necessary traction. Slick, full color pages, which became more and more in vogue as Sears became more affluent, were nearly useless. They would simply slide off and accomplish nothing. Fortunately at this critical point in our nation's history, commercial toilet tissue, 400 absorbent, nonskid sheets to a roll, became widely available at a quite reasonable price.

There were also other paper items in general use. Peach wrappers, the tissue in which peaches were wrapped for shipment from orchards, were a premium material. On the other hand, newsprint was generally shunned because the paper was inferior and the ink had a tendency to transfer from the paper to the body and thence to one's underwear.

In emergencies, people tended to use whatever was available. Once when my friend Bob Rogers was camping with his family, he found himself in the woods without tissue. With his trousers at his knees, he cast about for relief, finally plucking a cluster of leaves from nearby shrubs. While solving the immediate problem, he created a new one. The following week he was in agony with an acute outbreak of poison ivy.

Guiding light

Illumination and climate can have an impact on outhouse efficiency. While a flashlight or lantern may suffice for the limited vacation visit, more permanent light may be installed by running a wire from the home to the outhouse roof and thence inside to an electric fixture. Similarly, an electric heater is sometimes hooked up with a switch in the house so when the urge strikes, the switch may be flipped and the outhouse preheated before visitation. Where electricity is not available, a battery-powered lantern used in conjunction with a portable catalytic heater offers similar amenities.

Cold feet aren't really the problem

In areas where winters may be severe, there is often the problem of the cold seat. Leave it to the Alaskans to come up with a solution. From our most northern state, by way of a government forester visiting friends in Blackduck, Minnesota, we gained this bit of vital information: Make the seat out of Styrofoam. Fishing guides Harry and Mary Lambirth have a brand new outhouse at Blackduck with a Styrofoam seat that transmits no cold; indeed, it reflects only body heat. While such seats are not on the market commercially, it is no great chore nor expense to obtain a 24-inch square of one-inch styrofoam, cut it to the correct shape, sand it for a smooth fit and install it.

Full house

Lastly, a signal may be installed so a user may notify someone approaching that the facility is occupied. Some government biffies and portable satellites have a clever door latch that shows the word "Occupied" when in use. Wooden outhouses may be equipped with a simple device such as a movable arrow pointing to "Use" or "Vacant" as the case may be. Some folk have taken to placing a small American flag in a holder on the door to indicate occupancy, a rather touching show of patriotism.

Carpentry

On firm foundation grounded

The bases of the one-, two- and three-holers should rest on solid timbers such as 6x6s or 4x4s, which are cut about a foot longer than the planned outhouse floor. These timbers form the base but also provide a skid to which a chain or cable may be hooked to slide the outhouse to a new site when the original hole becomes filled. It pays to plan ahead. The neophyte has no idea how fast a hole will fill up, especially in use by several kids and perhaps a number of relatives or visitors.

However, there are builders out in the Kansas, Nebraska and Oklahoma tornado country who insist the facility must be securely anchored to the ground. Some of these builders extend corner timbers three or four feet below the floor and use extensive interior cross-bracing. It has always been our understanding that it is best to vacate the outhouse in a tornado and head for the home basement, storm cellar or at least a deep ditch. Outhouses are often the first things to blow away, along with chicken coops. There could be nothing much scarier than being caught in an outhouse when a tornado strikes.

ONE OF OUR CORRESPONDENTS in the west said he knew of a farmer who just got settled in his privy when a twister struck and picked up the unit. He was reported to have come down shaken but unscathed less than a mile away, just in time to complete the paper work.

As noted earlier, the hole should be a half foot smaller on each side than the actual outhouse. This allows the timbers to be set on solid ground and not over space. The timbers are levelled not only side to side but also with each other and cross pieces of the same 4x4 or 6x6 material spiked in place to provide the overall four-foot width. A longitudinal double 2x4 floor joist runs from side to side half the distance from the front. The floor, 3/4 plywood or planking, is nailed in place from the front timber to the joist. Strips of the same material are cut to length and used to shim the back half of the sides and the rear. This allows the wall plate to rest evenly all around.

The frame-up   Next, the back wall studs are cut and spiked to the upper and lower plates on 16-inch centers. The back wall frame is then lifted and spiked to the floor, then plumbed and held in place with 2x4 outside braces. The front wall frame and door frame are constructed, raised, plumbed and braced. Double studs are used at the sides and top of the door frame. The side walls are framed with the upper plate angled to accommodate the roof slope, front to back, and those frames raised. If the roof is of the peak variety, all walls are the same height and can be built and spiked directly into place.

A roof over your head   Most builders seek to get the roof in place before finishing the sidewalls in order to shelter the interior from rain. This is good planning. With the roof on, the interior can be handled in a more leisurely manner. Rafters may be 2x4s on 24-inch centers, nailed in place and sheathed with plywood. Trim boards add a nice touch and provide a firm edge for roofing. Shingles or roll roofing completes the roof cover. If a vent pipe is installed, flashing should cover the vent pipe exit.

The frame containing the toilet seats should be installed before the side walls are sheathed, just for convenience and ease of handling materials. The 2x4 seat frame is nailed to the back wall studs, supported in front and on the sides. The front splash board is spiked in place and the seat cover nailed down. Some builders saw the seat holes before nailing on the seat cover, some after. It's builder's choice.

Of course, you'll need walls

Half-inch exterior plywood provides excellent side-wall sheathing. On the Economy One-Holer, this is all the wall necessary. For more ambitious facilities, the plywood makes an excellent base for vertical board-and-batten, horizontal siding or any other finish material. Vinyl siding adds a crisp touch.

The best way to hang the door is to build the door and frame as a unit with the door on the hinges and the door knob in place. Door frames must be cut to fit inside the rough opening so care must be taken to measure precisely.

Some people paint their outhouses, some just leave them natural wood. If you figure to live more than 15 years and want the outhouse to last as long as you do, give it two coats of exterior paint or wood preservative.

SOME PEOPLE, LIKE OUR FRIENDS Nancy and Marty Lakner, paint the outhouse a different color every year just to provide a note of cheery brightness and variety at their summer cottage on the lake.

The Lakners have a spring cleanup ritual, inviting friends and relatives to come out on a weekend and rake leaves, gather and stack brush for burning, all in a sort of picnic atmosphere. One spring it became apparent that the old outhouse was on its last legs, sagging woefully and ready to cave in. The cleanup crew piled the leaves, brush and deadfalls against the back wall and set it on fire.

"A strange thing occurred," noted Nancy. "All those years of adding coat after coat of different colored paint created a finish that went up in flames in a variety of brilliant colors."

She went on to say that as the multi-hued flames licked at the back wall, the work crew took turns running inside, one at a time, to drop their pants, sit down and have their photos taken in the conflagration. Nobody got burned.

PETE DAVIS AND HIS WIFE, who live out at Eagle's Nest Lake, tell about building an outhouse in their basement in Duluth. They drew up some plans, purchased the lumber and built the outhouse one wall at a time. Then it was carried outside and assembled in the yard.

Pete says a neighbor came over for a look and inquired as to what he was doing. Pete told him it was a backup system in case the Duluth water supply ran out. "You can't do that," said the neighbor and walked away.

Pete and his son borrowed a snowmobile trailer, loaded the outhouse on it and drove 100 miles north to the cabin on Eagle's Nest Lake. His only regret is that he tried to get his wife to sit inside and toss out ribbons of toilet paper as they sped up Rt. 53, which she declined to do.

The first winter the temperature went down to 30 below so Pete installed a heat lamp inside, which was quite welcome on cold days. He says "25 years later the building stands, proud and sturdy" and is still useful whenever they have a power outage and the indoor plumbing cannot be used.

(Architect's note: If any of the foregoing information on building is not clear, you probably don't know a doggone thing about wood working and should hire a carpenter.)

Out with the old, in with the new. But wait! Which one stays?

Blueprints for 4x4 Economy One-Holer

Award-winning design by Steven H. McNeill, A.S.O.A

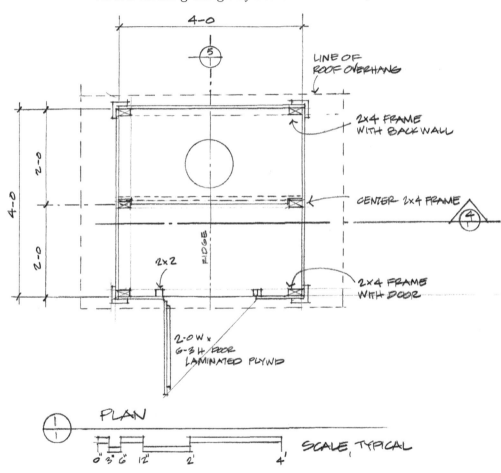

4-0

5

LINE OF
ROOF OVERHANG

2x4 FRAME
WITH BACK WALL

CENTER 2x4 FRAME

4

2-0

4-0

2-0

RIDGE

2x2

2x4 FRAME
WITH DOOR

2-0 W x
6-3 H DOOR
LAMINATED PLYWD

PLAN

1
1

0" 3" 6" 12"   2'   4'

SCALE, TYPICAL

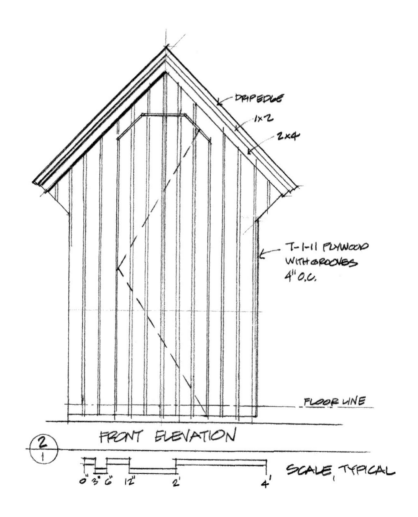

DRIP EDGE

1x2

2x4

T-1-11 PLYWOOD
WITH GROOVES
4" O.C.

FLOOR LINE

FRONT ELEVATION

2/1

0" 3" 6" 12"   2'   4'

SCALE, TYPICAL

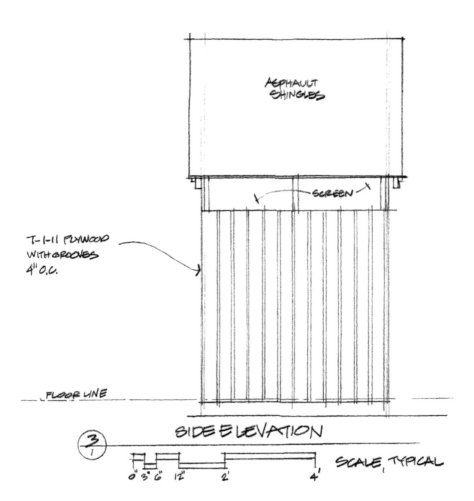

ASPHAULT
SHINGLES

SCREEN

T-1-11 PLYWOOD
WITH GROOVES
4" O.C.

FLOOR LINE

SIDE ELEVATION

3
1

0" 3" 6" 12"   2'   4'

SCALE, TYPICAL

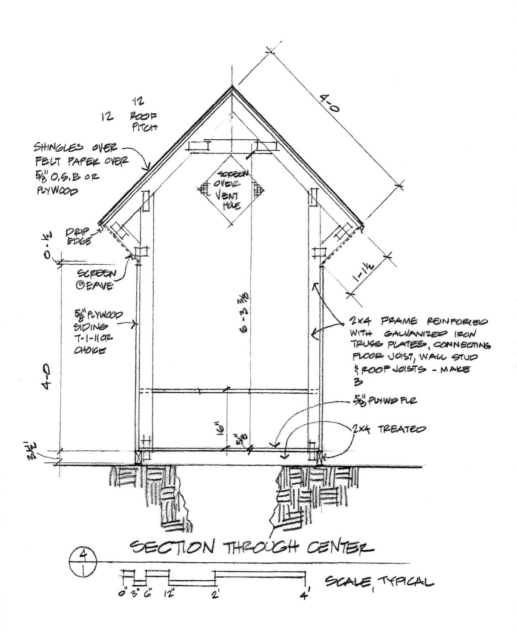

12
12 ROOF
     PITCH

4'-0

SHINGLES OVER
FELT PAPER OVER
5/8" O.S.B OR
PLYWOOD

SCREEN
OVER
VENT
HOLE

DRIP
EDGE

0-6

SCREEN
@ EAVE

1-1½

6'-3 3/10

5/8" PLYWOOD
SIDING
T-1-11 OR
CHOICE

2X4 FRAME REINFORCED
WITH GALVANIZED IRON
TRUSS PLATES, CONNECTING
FLOOR JOIST, WALL STUD
& ROOF JOISTS - MAKE
3

4'-0

5/8" PLYWD FLR

16"

5/8

2X4 TREATED

3½"

SECTION THROUGH CENTER

4
1

0" 3" 6" 12"   2'   4'   SCALE, TYPICAL

51

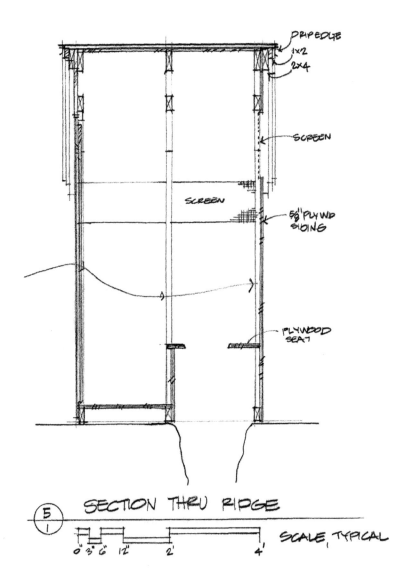

DRIPEDGE

1x2

2x4

SCREEN

SCREEN

5/8" PLYWD SIDING

PLYWOOD SEAT

SECTION THRU RIDGE

5/1

0" 3" 6" 12"   2'   4'

SCALE, TYPICAL

The Knot Hole Gang

Anyone who ever attended a country school knows that the rowdier male element was ever curious about what went on in the outhouse designated "Girls." There is scarcely a rural school in the nation without its own sniggering jest involving the girl's toilet with a knot hole in back, or a small hole drilled, where morally deficient male students were apt to sneak up for a peek when the facility was occupied. In most school yards, there were two toilets several paces apart and it was worth a pasting from the principal to be spotted loitering in the vicinity of the girl's unit. But the threat of corporal punishment failed to deter the bolder roughnecks, usually the same ones who crept behind the boy's facility to smoke prohibited cigarettes. In grandma's day, some countermeasures could be taken such as keeping a long, peeled willow branch in the girl's outhouse that could be suddenly jammed through any aperture where a suspected voyeur might be peering. A scream of anguish and a swelling, blackening eye was vengeance enough.

However, with the inevitable progress of modern times, the preferred weapon of female defense became the can of spray paint kept handy near the seat. I cannot vouch for the following incident, but it seems probable and was related by a young lady of impeccable character.

IT SEEMS that she became aware, through the older boys smirking and snickering, that some of them were engaged in illicit observation through a knot hole waist-high in the girls' facility. My informant, a 12-year-old, had just entered the unit when she was warned by a shrill whistle from a classmate that a boy had approached from the back. Going about her business as usual to keep the attention of the peeker, she calmly reached over, picked up the aerosol paint can, put the nozzle against the hole and cut loose. Blinded, the bully staggered back with howls of pain as the aerosol began to smart. In addition, every kid in school knew what he had done from the big splotch of black paint around his eye. Mortification, however, turned to anger and when school let out, the offender intercepted her outside school and threatened bodily harm. The young lady quickly removed her right shoe, grasped the toe and flexed the heel like a weapon.

"What happened to you with the paint can," she hissed, "is nothing compared to what I'll do to you if you even try to get close to me." She reported there were no further problems.

Just general good maintenance of outhouses requires keeping all openings filled, not particularly to discourage peepers, but to prevent invasion by various noxious creatures, which brings us to the next segment of this book: Creepy Crawly Things.

Creepy Crawly Things

A little spray goes a long way

While on the subject of spray cans, perhaps a word concerning insecticides would be appropriate. Little creatures with legs and wings, not to mention equipment to bite with, like to get inside the outhouse to make life miserable for visitors. Most immediate and pesky are spring blackflies followed closely by mosquitoes. A can of Raid will usually eliminate this problem. Of more long term concern are wasps, which may infest the premises and construct large nests. When sufficiently irritated, these stinging creatures may come after any person nearby, inflicting extremely painful stings. It pays to spray the nest thoroughly, pacify the inhabitants and destroy the nest.

Spiders are known to take up residence in outhouses, but are more entertaining than irritating. There is something restful and soothing about sitting with your elbows on your knees, chin in palms, watching a spider go about its business of web spinning, fly catching or simply hanging on the shrouds watching whomever is watching back.

A lot of insect matters can be overcome by application of an ordinary fly swatter. A well equipped outhouse should have one hanging on a nail within easy reach.

Ticks are tough

A more serious problem involves ticks, which do not respond to swats. There are two varieties of these noxious pests: wood ticks and deer ticks.

Normally, they are found in the leaf litter in yard and forest, but they occasionally invade outhouses where they lie in ambush on the undersides of the seats, seeking to dine on someone's warm torso. Deer ticks are tiny, like the head of a pin but can inflict a wound that may result in the transmission of debilitating Lyme disease. Inspection of one's body, or parts thereof, should be done regularly when spending time in the woods.

The same applies to wood ticks, which are larger and uglier although their bite is not as damaging. Wood ticks are flat, brown, like a bran crumb with legs. Ticks like to bury their heads under one's epidermis and suck blood, a rather repulsive activity. Wood tick bites may become infected and create problems.

DOCTORS KNOW all about handling tick bites, both deer ticks and wood ticks. Two physicians in our area who are versed in tick damage are the Doctors Bianco, Joe and Mary. Joe is my regular physician. Some time back when I had a tick bite me in a rather delicate place, a bite that became infected, I headed for the clinic post haste.

"What can we do for you?" inquired the young lady at the desk.

"Well, I...uh...have this tick bite that is infected."

"Uh huh. Let's see. Oh, Dr. Bianco is on duty."

"Fine. I have a lot of confidence in Dr. Bianco."

Moments later a nurse directed me to an examining room

and told me to drop my pants. This was accomplished and shortly thereafter, as I stood half naked, Dr. Bianco came in. Imagine my surprise to discover it was not Dr. Joe Bianco but Dr. Mary Bianco. As I hastily attempted to cover my nakedness, Dr. Mary, with professional coolness, explained that she was well acquainted with the human body, gender notwithstanding.

"Let's have a look," she said.

The problem of the tick bite was taken care of with dispatch, but my embarrassment lingered for some time. If nothing else, I achieved some measure of appreciation for the discomfort women must feel when they are inspected in detail by male doctors.

Maintenance

The nose knows

A person can determine immediately if an outhouse has been properly designed and maintained. The nose makes that assessment. If properly built, with correct venting, odor is held to a minimum. Old timers kept a bag or tin of lime in the corner of the outhouse. A generous scoop of lime down the hole after the job was finished kept the aroma to an acceptable level.

In the short term, a spray can of bathroom deodorant is a worthwhile accessory. Lavender or Old Spice lend a nice touch.

Queen of clean

Good housekeeping may require a thorough interior cleaning about once every two weeks or so. A large bucket of hot water to which a couple tablespoons of bleach have been added assures cleanliness. The hot water is applied to walls, seat, splash board and floor with a vigorously wielded broom. Tidy folk also scrub the underside of the seat around the hole every two weeks, more often if young children are involved or if a family member has been attacked with some intestinal malady.

In any case, if bleach is used in the water, the seat area should be rinsed off with plain water and carefully dried before used. Bleach coming in contact with human skin can create a painful mark.

There are, of course, a number of modern commercial bathroom cleaners that do an adequate job. Back in grandfather's day, when going to town for supplies was a major undertaking, soaps, cleaners and various nostrums were supplied to farm dwellers by itinerant salesmen such as those dispensing Watkins products. In our area, the Watkins Man was held in as high esteem as the family doctor or church pastor.

MY OLD FRIEND, the late Frank Kirman, who farmed some 780 acres of corn and meadow near Lockport, Illinois, told a story about the Watkins Man, an incident for which I have no verification, but pass along as an example of rural Americana:

It seems that the Watkins Man, according to Frank, had been assailed with a bowel problem and had dosed up with a laxative just before breakfast. As he began making his morning rounds in his product-laden Model T, he became aware that the physic was beginning to work.

He was in a somewhat remote area, explained Frank, where the farms were some distance apart, and as his discomfort became more acute, he thought of leaping out and seeking relief in the roadside ditch. However, a frantic glance around the car interior convinced him that he had sold his entire supply of toilet tissue. At that point he spied a farm on the horizon, accelerated the Model T and raced to the buildings ahead. He swung into the yard in a cloud of dust, leaped from the vehicle and ran toward the farmer who was busy by the corner of the house sawing firewood.

"Where is your outhouse?" yelled the now desperate Watkins Man.

"Right around the corner," the farmer pointed a finger.

The Watkins Man put on a burst of speed and shot

around the corner. Unfortunately, there was clothes line stretched from the house to a nearby tree, at forehead height. In his haste, the Watkins Man smacked into the clothes line, was upended and landed in the dust.

"Oh, dear," the farmer cried in dismay. "I forgot to tell you about the clothes line."

"Oh, that's all right," said the pale Watkins Man as he slowly struggled to his feet. "I don't think I would have made it anyway."

Only for the use intended The occasional outhouse user has the bad habit of throwing trash down the hole in the outhouse. Honey dippers, the men who clean cess pools and outhouses for a living, find all manner of extraneous material from baseballs to whiskey bottles, old toys, magazines and kitchen utensils. It should be impressed on every family member that no foreign substances should go down the hole. Most of this stuff is not biodegradable and will simply not go away. Furthermore, it can be dangerous.

GRANDFATHER LIKED TO TELL about his neighbor to the east, Otto Stuebler. Of German ancestry, Otto was a hardworking farmer and a pillar in the Lutheran church.

One Saturday, Otto's wife Lena was dry cleaning the old man's blue serge suit for Sunday wear and when finished, dumped the remaining dry cleaner down the outhouse hole. As she returned to the kitchen, Otto came out of the cow barn in rather a hurry, rushed to the outhouse, seated himself and stoked his briar with pipe tobacco, as was his habit. He struck a match, lit the pipe and hurled the match down the hole.

From within the kitchen Lena heard this gosh-awful explosion. She rushed out into the backyard to see bits of lumber, shingles and toilet paper coming down from the sky. Otto rose up from the wreckage, shaking his head as Lena rushed to his aid.

"What happened, Otto?" Lena cried.

"I don't know," said the bewildered old man. "It must've been something I ate."

Vandals and Pranksters

No dumping allowed Many outhouses, since the time of recorded history or perhaps even before, have been victims of outhouse vandals. There are, unfortunately, among some of the less-cultured juvenile elements of our society, some despicable individuals who consider the height of humor is the dumping over of their neighbor's outhouse. Such activity usually occurs on Halloween when groups of undisciplined urchins are apt to roam the countryside after dark, seeking to engage in some manner of mischief. The more ruthless of these delinquents will crouch unseen in the shadows waiting for a resident to emerge from the house in a more or less urgent response to a natural function. Once it is determined the outhouse is duly occupied, the vandals stealthily approach, place their weight against the back wall and tip the unit over on its door. It requires little imagination to picture the frantic plight of the terrorized individual inside the pitch black facility.

SUCH WAS THE EXPERIENCE of our neighbor, Old Man Martin, a crabby individual with an artificial leg, courtesy of the German army in World War I. Every youngster within a mile despised the old man who reciprocated by brandishing a rake and swearing vile oaths at any kid who cut across a corner of his property. One Halloween, a half dozen juvenile delinquents dumped Old

Man Martin's toilet building with the old man inside. The screams of rage and profanity were wondrous to hear. Indeed, it was such a satisfactory escapade that the perpetrators determined to try again the following year.

On Halloween, they again crept to the edge of the old man's property and hid in the dark behind a clump of raspberry bushes. A kerosene lamp shone light from the kitchen window, and an occasional moving shadow indicated the old man was home. However, an hour went by and the victim failed to appear. At length, the perpetrators decided he was not coming out, so they tiptoed up to dump the empty outhouse anyway. What they did not know was that Old Man Martin had anticipated their appearance and earlier in the day had hooked a winch to the front of the facility, pulling it three feet forward and exposing the pit. You already know what happened. As the six-member assault team stalked forward in the dark to put their shoulders against the back wall, the first three fell headlong into the pit. Gagging and coughing, they managed to climb out and retreat post haste to the alley behind one of their homes where they were thoroughly hosed down. So far as I can recall, no one ever again vandalized Old Man Martin's outhouse.

The teleportation trick Vandalism may sometimes take other forms. Larger groups of delinquents, perhaps eight or ten, have been known to tip an outhouse over backward so the door stays shut, pick it up like pall bearers, carry it to another destination and set it back upright. Thus outhouses have appeared at busy traffic intersections, the front porches of sedate sorority houses, or the yards of village churches. The latter was considered particularly effective if Halloween fell on Saturday night so the outhouse would be waiting when the congregation arrived for worship services on Sunday morning. The foregoing, and similar incidents, aptly illustrate the depraved character of those who engage in such activities.

OUR OLD FRIEND Pete Zebich tells us about a Winton couple who had friends over to their cabin on Fall Lake. The ladies went berry picking while the men stayed home, played cribbage and demolished a jug of Old Tennis Shoe. They happened to see a bear cruising the yard, shot it, posed it on the seat of the outhouse and shut the door. When the women came back they had to visit the toilet. When they opened the door and saw the bear they screamed. The guys nonchalantly told them to be patient, that the bear would probably take care of his business quickly.

NUGENT'S RESORT was a source of hilarity in the old days. They had a speaker installed under the seat in the outhouse and when one of the female guests would enter, they would wait perhaps ten seconds and then reach for the microphone. The guest would come flying out of the outhouse, pants at half mast, when a voice below her would say: "Would you mind moving over, lady? We're trying to paint down here."

Ode to Fort Necessity

Your weathered walls of grainy wood
    Your roof with rafters bent,
Your seat of old familiar feel
    A solace when we went.

In memory I see you yet,
    Your door ajar with greeting,
Beckoning to those in need
    Of sanctuary seating.

I've trod your path
    Through winter's snows
And autumn's colored leaves
    Harked as summer's violent storms
Whistled past your eaves.

We've named you Fort Necessity,
    A staunch and firm redoubt,
Assailed by claps of thunder
    From within as well as out.

Oh, outhouse brave and rugged,
    Withstanding fortune's blows,
A sanctuary for those in need,
    A bastion of repose.

"Jackpine Bob" Cary

About the Author

Bob Cary, known across the Northland as "Jackpine Bob," was born in Joliet, Illinois, on October 20, 1921. He was raised in the farm country, attended public schools, and had finished Community College when WWII broke out. He enlisted in the U.S. Marines and served in combat from 1942 to 1945 with the 2nd Division. He returned to civilian life and attended the Chicago Academy of Fine Art for two years, then went to work as a writer and illustrator. Bob worked for the *Joliet Herald-News*, *Joliet Spectator*, and as outdoor editor of the *Chicago Daily News* and the *Ely Echo*. Bob currently is a columnist at the *Mesabi Daily News*. He has seven books in print and countless magazine articles published. He has illustrated both his own and other authors' books, and owns an art gallery in Ely. Bob owned and operated a canoe outfitting and guiding service for eight years at Ely. He is currently president of the American Society of Outhouse Architects.

"Jackpine Bob" Cary